# WRITE A COLLECTION OF POETRY IN A YEAR

BUILD YOUR COLLECTION, A POEM AT A TIME...

HOW-TO BOOKS FOR WRITERS

M V FRANKLAND

# FOREWORD

Write a Collection of Poetry in a Year

Write a poem every week, let your verse begin to speak.

# INTRODUCTION

There are many people who aspire to produce a collection of poetry, and there is no doubt about what a tremendous accomplishment it is. However, many would-be poets say 'I wouldn't know how to approach it,' or 'I never finish anything I start' as reasons *why* they never begin. Another reason I hear is 'I'm not good enough,' or ' no one would want to read my poems.' I promise that this course will dispel those fears!

This book is derived from a class-taught course that has been tried and tested by many poets, and ensured they go from the planning process through to the hugely enjoyable creation of poem after poem, towards completion of that all-important first draft.

This book, as well as supporting the creation of your poetry collection, will develop your craft as a poet. In addition, it will give you the tools needed to polish your first draft until it is good enough to be published. I write this as both a published poet, and as a creative writing teacher with an MA in Creative Writing. There are publications that promise a completed collection in less time than a year, but speaking from experience, I know that a year is a realistic time frame.

The book has been divided into twenty nine sections with a view to around a fortnight being spent on each section, once you have gone beyond the introductory sections. Of course, you can approach and complete each section as quickly or as slowly as you need to. Where examples are required, I will either exemplify a technique or form with my own writing, or signpost you to something freely available online.

Underpinning this book is the requirement to write at least one poem every fortnight, which will result in a pamphlet size collection in a year. However, one poem per week will ensure completion of an impressive full length, fifty two poem collection at the end of the year. You can complete your poetry collection using this book as your guide, but there is also a companion workbook available to support the tasks and activities and give you space to reflect and to plan. Wherever you see [cwb] (companion workbook,) in the text, you will know there is a section in the accompanying workbook for you to write in.

Completion of your collection might be the dream and I promise you there is no feeling like holding your published collection in your hands. At the time of writing, I am working on my third full-length poetry collection. But the journey is just as enjoyable and rewarding as the destination. So enjoy every minute and I look forward to helping you all the way from planning to publication.

# 1

## GENERATING IDEAS

WELCOME to the start of your exciting journey as a poet! I can't wait to support you from beginning to end and to help you achieve what is probably a long-held dream. So start by making a commitment to yourself that you will complete this course!

If you were taking this course in one of my face-to-face groups, or online, we would be doing one section every fortnight, but because this is a book, you can go as fast or as slow as you like.

I worked alone to write my own first poetry collection, which as a result, took me three years in total, after a lot of getting it out and putting it away again. But having being able to refine my process allows me now to pass on the way to do it in one year. It is possible to work on one section per week and do double the amount of poems – you will, of course, then finish in six months!

This first section is dedicated to you planning the poetry you want to write. Responding to the questions will set you on the right path.

Being a reader of poetry is important, as much of what you read will permeate your own writing and increase the number of 'tools' you have in your 'writer's toolbox.'

Your responses will help you give yourself the time and space to develop a writing habit and focus on what inspires and interests you.

[cwb1.1] **Yourself: The Reader**

Which poet do you most admire? Why?

What is your all-time favourite poem? What makes it stand out?

[cwb1.2] **Yourself: The Poet**

Why do you want to write a collection of poetry? *There could be several reasons.*

What has stood in the way of you starting this so far? *Advice and support will be provided along the way to overcome known obstacles that get in the way of many writers.*

What place can you give yourself to write? *You may be lucky enough to have your own desk or may need to carve out a place.*

What improvements can you make to this space? *For example, a picture, a candle, lighting, music, etc.*

Is there a time of day when you can usually devote half an hour to yourself and your writing?

What unique experiences/events/settings have you lived through? *Drawing on what is familiar is a brilliant place to start.*

At this stage, have you any ideas of what the poetry collection might be about that is trying to get out of you? *Don't worry if not – lots of support will be offered to help you to generate your initial idea.*

Are you drawn towards any of the following themes or topics?

- Love
- War/Peace
- Travel
- Seasons
- Natural World

- Water (sea, etc)
- Family
- Change
- Childhood Difficulties
- Humour
- Growing older
- Issues
- Horror/Supernatural
- Spiritual
- Child/Teenage
- A Hobby
- The Garden

Do you have any thoughts/preferences around rhyme, (or not,) structural or free verse?

Make a brief list of your life experiences under the headings: *Happy/Sad/Other.*

What places have you been? (visits, holidays, work.)

*Choose the most significant.*

*How did it make you feel?*

*What did you hear? See? Do?*

What other descriptions could you give to someone who has not been there?

Who has had the most impact on you? *Think of someone ...*

- *Funny*
- *Optimistic*
- *Inspirational*
- *Depressive*
- *Chaotic*

What would you like to leave of yourself? What is your most important message?

Who might you write for? You might say *anyone and everyone* but it's an advantage if you have got a target audience in mind.

Careful consideration of the above factors should be starting to give you some ideas around the theme and content of the poems you will soon be writing. Hopefully, after answering the above questions, you're now raring to go! In preparation for continuing you might want to:

1. Buy yourself a 'special' A4 notebook and pen which you will keep only for your poetry – make it a hardback one with a design you love.
2. Begin carrying a notebook and pen around with you at all times – writers notice things or should I say – writers are nosy! You never know when you will overhear a conversation or see something, perhaps in the landscape that could be the spark of a poem.
3. Make one observation each day as you go about your life. This should be something sensory. Write a few lines about each observation. You do not need to do anything more with this just yet, (unless you want to!) At this stage, you are getting in the habit of noticing things and capturing them in your notebook.
4. Find a copy of your favourite poem.

2

—————

# THE VITAL INGREDIENTS OF A POEM

THINK of the type of poems you enjoy reading. As previously mentioned, you should read as much poetry as you can whilst doing this course. Although I do think that being writers somehow interrupts us as readers. I find that now I write professionally, I am less accepting of anything I read and am always reading beyond the lines.

You should find, however, that the techniques you come across in your reading will infiltrate your own writing and make you a better poet.

**Re-read your favourite poem and consider the following questions:** [cwb 2.1]

1. What do you consider to be good about the poem? (or not.)
2. Does it 'invite' you in?
3. Is it engaging? Are you compelled to read to the end?
4. Does it resonate with you after you have read it?
5. What patterns or structures does it have? (if any.)

. . .

There are no right or wrong answers. It is your own opinion that matters. It is important that whilst you are compiling your own poetry collection, you continue to read a variety of different poems, developing your skill of reading deeply and considering how the poet has constructed their work.

Below is a list of 'ingredients' which will help you write the perfect poem. Perhaps they are contained within the poem you have chosen as your favourite. You should refer to this list as you continue with the course. You might also notice as you progress through this book how much I like lists!

**An arresting title** – A title that's original and encapsulates the poem, without being too abstract.

**An attention grabbing first line** – This is where a reader is hooked, either by asking a question or piquing curiosity.

**Starts in the right place** – Often, the first draft of a poem offers unnecessary backstory or scene setting. At second draft stage, explore what might happen if you 'cut' the first few lines. Would the poem be weaker or stronger?

**Fires the imagination** – Let the reader do some work. Don't offer all the information to them, let them fill in gaps and draw their own conclusions.

. . .

**Tells a story** – A good poem should take the reader on a journey and have them moving from the starting point to the end. A change or shift should take place.

**Offers new description and imagery** – an original metaphor or simile is always memorable. Poems should also allow for readers to experience them through the senses.

**Takes a look at something differently** – a fresh approach makes for a memorable poem, whilst exploring a new angle or question.

**Offers something unexpected or surprising** – this could be a change of opinion or direction or maybe a twist towards the end.

**Audibly pleasing** - rhyme or half rhyme should be original and appear effortless and uncontrived. If writing in free verse, internal rhyme and the use of alliteration could be used. Within this, the pace of the poem could be considered. Long vowel sounds slow it down, whilst short vowels and monosyllabic words speed it up.

**Understandable** – poetry should be accessible and allow for the reader to interpret it in their own way. Whilst writing ambiguously can be thought and discussion-provoking, if something is too abstract, it may be difficult for a reader to find a way into it.

**Offers contrast** – balance is often a factor within a poem – light/dark, happiness/sadness, differing opinions, other possibilities.

**Ends in the right place** – A good poem should not allow the ending to rumble on once a conclusion has been reached.

**Offers a final line which resonates** – the last line should resonate and be memorable. Allow it to draw the poem to a close but leave the reader wishing there was more.

3

———

# THE VITAL INGREDIENTS
# OF A POETRY COLLECTION

IN THE LAST section you chose a poem, now I would like you to choose a poetry *collection* which appeals to you.

This can be full length, (fifty plus poems,) or pamphlet size, (nineteen to twenty five poems.)

Whilst browsing through it, pay special attention to the first and last poems in order to think about the following questions. [cwb3.1]

1. What is the theme of the collection?
2. Does the first poem draw you in?
3. Does the final poem leave resonance?
4. What is the poet's style – is it mixed?
5. Would you recommend the collection to others? Why?

Yes, it's another list! Below is a list of 'ingredients' needed for the perfect poetry collection. Perhaps they are contained within

9

the collection you have chosen. You should keep referring to this list as you make progress with your own collection.

**A theme or thread** – Ideally, a collection of poetry should have a theme or thread that loosely or firmly holds it all together. This could be something concrete like motherhood, landscape or ageing.

**An arresting title** - A title needs to capture the reader's attention. It is a good idea that you have at least a 'working title.' This will ensure that your collection is a tangible product as you continue working on it.

**An initial poem that hooks the reader in** – All the poems will have earned their place in a collection but the first poem needs to engage the reader and set the tone for it.

**Something unique** – Most poems and themes for collections have been done before, a good collection should find a way to be different, have a different slant or way of dealing with its topic.

**Poems that use auditory devices** - rhyme, half rhyme and internal rhyme, also alliteration, onomatopoeia (words that sounds like their meaning such as buzz and hiss,) and short and long vowel sounds.

·  ·  ·

**Poems that are visually pleasing** – shape poems or poems that sit centrally or symmetrically on the page, not too much dense text and split into manageable stanzas.

I love sonnets for this reason. They're square and symmetrical – sorry to sound so geeky!

**A departing from the poet's own voice** – whilst poetry displays the poet's unique writing style and poetic voice, it should also offer accessibility for the reader who will want to make it their own and identify with it.

Allowing the reading experience to be active, and for the reader to make their own interpretations is something else to bear in mind.

This is an exciting aspect of being a writer – when you write a poem, it solely belongs to you, but when in the hands of a reader, you share it with them to make of it what they will.

**A final poem that offers resonance** – A collection should end with a thought-provoking echo. Something memorable that will stay with the reader.

**An overall message** – There should be a reason for the collection. What does it address? What message does it convey? What difference does the poetry make?

**A collection that offers a journey** – a beginning, middle and end within a collection. Is there a shift or a movement within it? Is there a transition between the start and end points?

**4**

---

# RHYTHM AND RHYME

LET'S start with some explanations of the terms used in this section.


**Rhyme** A repetition of similar sounds (or the same sound) in two or more words, most often in the final syllables of lines in poems.

    shines, dines

    June/tune

    desire/require


**Rhythm** The measured flow of words and phrases in verse or prose as determined by the relation of long and short or stressed and unstressed syllables.


In iambic pentameter, each line of *poetry* has 10 syllables that alternate in an unstressed, stressed rhythmic pattern. By stressed, I mean the emphasised part of the word when it is spoken. For example, *moment* - the emphasis is on the first syllable of the word.

Sonnets are written in iambic pentameter. Here are a couple of lines from one of Shakespeare's sonnets. (The stressed syllables are emboldened.)

My **mistress' eyes** are **nothing like** the **sun**
Coral is **far** more **red** than **her** lips' **red.**

**Half rhyme** A poetic device used more often in contemporary poetry. It is also called an **imperfect rhyme, slant rhyme, near rhyme** or **oblique rhyme.**

It can be defined as a **rhyme** in which the stressed syllables of ending consonants match, however the preceding vowel sounds do not match.

scrape/keep. (The same 'p' consonant sound is heard at the end of the words, yet the vowel sounds before that final sound differ.)

moon/run.
hold/bald.

You may want to find your own examples of poems, but here are two poems that investigate rhyme and rhythm – *Leisure* by William Henry Davies is available online and is written in full rhyme and iambic pentameter.

· · ·

*I am Vertical* by Sylvia Plath offers an example of half rhyme and is also available on the internet.

**Seek out either of the above poems or find your own before considering the following:** [cwb 4.1]

1. Can you describe the rhyming pattern within the poem?
2. Does it have a rhythm when read out loud?
3. What do you like about it?
4. What do you not like about it?
5. Can you relate to it?
6. Can you hear the poet's voice?
7. Does it have a movement within it?
8. What sort of poem do you prefer? Rhyme or half rhyme?

**To rhyme or not to rhyme!** This is the factor that possibly causes the most division amongst readers of poetry. Some people argue that a poem is 'not' a poem unless it rhymes. Others find rhyme outdated and contrived.

I would argue that rhyme has its place as long as it is as original and uncontrived as possible. This is why half-rhyme is a brilliant tool we have available to us in our writing toolbox.

But even when a poem is free verse, which we will soon be coming to, we have other devices at our disposal to deepen its poetic quality. We have assonance, consonance, imagery and repetition to name but a few. A poem should be audibly pleasing, as well as conjuring images through the use of original description.

I've heard the question, 'what makes a poem a poem?' My answer would be, because the poet who has written it says it's a poem! Nowadays, anything goes!

It's now time to plan and write the first poem for your collection...

[cwb 4.2] **Write a list of ten words** you would consider using in a poem which explores the theme of trees.

[cwb 4.3] **Write a poem** *as though you are a tree* so it will be in first person (I, me, my.) Before you start, respond to the following:

1. Where are you?
2. What have you seen or experienced as time has elapsed?
3. What is the season?
4. What is your significance?
5. What is the time of day?

The above planning offers a starting point, as opposed to starting to write without any prior consideration. It makes it much easier to find your way into the poem.

. . .

First draft your poem, choosing a rhyme scheme, (rhyme or half rhyme,) which also incorporates a rhythm, (tum-ti-tum-ti-tum-ti-tum-ti-tum,) when it is read aloud.

Remember that the first draft is just that, a first draft. You will return to your poem for editing later in the course. Initially you will be getting your thoughts down, and then organising them. The poem can be any length you choose.

The ten words you have listed previously are not allowed in your poem: if you have readily and easily thought of them, they are most likely overused in poetry. (You can of course, substitute them, and a thesaurus is great for this.)

Enjoy the process – the first draft stage is wonderful!

# 5

## THE HAIKU

I AM NOW GOING to present you with a short-form poetry activity. You can use haikus individually to divide up sections within your poetry collection or you can write a series of haikus, known as a haiku string.

The Haiku is a Japanese poetic form which has become popular in the UK, with several poetry competitions inviting them.

Haikus often imply a season and merge this with an aspect of nature. This lyric form of 17 syllables in 3 lines of 5, 7, 5, syllables emerged in the 16th century.

Flowers are waving (5)
    but don't demand attention. (7)
    They can simply be. (5)

. . .

**[cwb5.1] Choose a season, and an aspect of nature, then weave it into you own haiku.**

Haikus are a wonderful way of achieving completion of a poem in a short space of time. For this reason, they are one of my favourite poetic forms to write, and I've found that my writing students enjoy writing them too. It always amuses me, watching them count out the syllables on their fingers as they are creating them.

Once you have written your first haiku, focus on the other three seasons in order to achieve a 'haiku string' which offers a description for each season.

I hope you will find them as addictive as I do.

**6**

---

## THE TANKA

THE TANKA IS another Japanese form that is becoming more popular and offers slightly more space for content than the Haiku. And they are just as enjoyable!

It is a thirty-one-syllable poem, and is traditionally, but not always, written in a single unbroken line. It means "short song," and is known for its five-line, 5/7/5/7/7 syllable count form.

The tanka originated in the seventh century AD and became the preferred verse form not only in the Japanese Imperial Court, where nobles competed in tanka contests, but for women and men engaged in courtship.

The economy and suitability for emotional expression made it ideal for intimate communication; lovers would, after an evening spent together, (often clandestinely!) write a tanka to give to the other the next morning as a gift of gratitude. It is also widely used to convey the subject of nature.

Below are examples of two tanka, one about love, one about nature.


The first star I see (5)
>     invites me to make a wish (7)
>     that no one can know (5)
>     as within me stars will join (7)
>     and a dream may start to grow. (7)


Over the valley (5)
>     clouds jostle for position, (7)
>     I reach and touch them, (5)
>     tug each from the darkened sky (7)
>     and the sunshine reigns again. (7)


**Choose an aspect of nature for your first tanka [cwb 6.1] and an aspect of love, (perhaps the forbidden kind!) for your second, to write your two Tankas.**


The two subjects of *nature and love* can also be merged if you would like to write a third tanka.


As with the haiku, this is a lovely short form that will break up your collection and add variety. You can also present tankas as a string, so each tanka is offered as a verse.

# 7

# THE SONNET

THE SONNET IS my favourite poem ever. It has its own rules but once you have mastered them, you can break them. There's something aesthetically pleasing about its shape and symmetry on the page – gosh I'm showing off my nerdy side now!

It is a poem of an expressive thought or idea, made up of fourteen lines, each being ten syllables long. Its rhymes are arranged according to one of the following schemes.

*An English sonnet* (abab, cdcd, efef, gg)

The more common English sonnet has three quatrains, (verses of four lines,) followed by a two line rhyming couplet, using the line structure abab, cdcd, efef, gg. (The a's rhyme, the b's rhyme and so on.)

.  .  .

Here is an example:

**Our Mighty Fallen**


Seemingly evergreen, teeming with pride,
    showing the vibrant colours of their youth,
    ignorant yet of tears that will be cried;
    drenched in sunshine, overlooking the truth.
    Facing skies that impart memories of love,
    in darkness, only stars give company;
    sheltered by hope that's below and above,
    not shaken by what their eyes cannot see


Holding on steadfast, as fear starts to seize,
    watching the blackening clouds burst their rain,
    others in time start to drift from the trees,
    all brace themselves for the dread and the pain.
    Sinking through time and committed to ground,
    eternal darkness coils itself around.


*An Italian Sonnet* (abba abba cdecde)


The first eight lines (called an octave,) consist of two quatrains (four lines each,) and normally open the poem as the question.


These are followed by six lines (called a sestet) that reply to the question.

. . .

Note that the end rhyme schemes alter in each verse.

Here is an example:

**Dread**

<u>Octave</u>

Having to wait is difficult to do,
 for results that could change the course of life.
 An outcome hinged on the edge of a knife,
 answers that mean he may not make it through.
 It's tugging him down, he's anxious and blue,
 will illness cheat him of wedding his wife?
 never has he stared at this kind of strife,
 a helplessness that, to him, is so new.

<u>**Sestet**</u>

Yet perhaps it's been caught early enough
 or maybe there'll be nothing there at all,
 from then, each moment, he'll appreciate,
 knowing things can be worse when time feels tough.
 He'll cherish each chance of life's rise and fall,
 enjoying the now, before it's too late.

. . .

Sonnets often present an 'argument' or different viewpoints which can be very subtle. This makes them a very versatile form of poetry.

Tightest is the 14 line structure, ten syllables and a 'turn' at the start of line 9, but nowadays there are lots of variations and many poets consider that they have written a sonnet, simply if they have written a fourteen line poem.

*The 'turn' means a subtle change in tone, mood or opinion.*

[cwb7.1] **Now write your own sonnet, using the following framework.** Jot a line of notes down in response to each of the following prompts. Do not worry yet about syllables or rhyme – this is the planning stage.

Within your sonnet you are going to mull something over before coming to a conclusion.

Think about a situation or event you are anticipating, perhaps apprehensively. Bring to mind what you are/were worrying about. You can do this 'retrospectively' if more suitable. Alternatively, you could use this two-part structure to mull over a decision that needs to be made or to explore two sides of an argument.

. . .

**Lines 1 and 2:** What is the situation or event you are anticipating? Briefly sum up its importance in your life.

**Lines 3 and 4:** What or who is weighing negatively on what is to come?

**Lines 5 and 6:** What is the worst thing that could possibly happen?

**Lines 7 and 8:** How is all this making you feel?

**Lines 9 and 10:** Starting with the word 'yet' 'but' or 'so' as a pivotal word, present the best case scenario that could happen.

**Lines 11 and 12:** How would this make you feel? What would be the effects (near and far-reaching?)

**Lines 13 and 14:** How do you feel now and what has been the benefit of thinking this through?


[cwb7.2] **Next, weave your notes into lines of ten syllables,** introducing rhyme, with a couplet at the end. You could aim for either the English or the Italian version, or you could write in rhyming couplets.


Let your sonnet rest for a couple of days, then go back and polish it up, making sure that every word is the best it can be. We will be looking more closely at editing later in the course. Sonnets are a great addition to any collection and if you enjoy performing your poetry, more on that later, they are fairly easy to memorise for performance.

**8**

---

# FREE VERSE

'FREE VERSE' is poetry without any defined pattern of rhyme or rhythm. It is sometimes called 'narrative poetry.'

The example below falls into this category – it has no rhyme or rhythm but does employ some poetic devices, such as repeated sounds, words and verse structure.

You could refer to the 'ingredients of a perfect poem' list earlier in the book, for a reminder of some of these devices.

There is a wonderful freedom in free verse, as the name implies.

There is no restriction or rules, but still we need to remember those all important 'ingredients!'

.   .   .

**When Someone has Loved You**


It's not until someone is no longer there
    that you really come to know them.
    Recalling their wisdom,
    remembering their words,
    their echo around you.


It's not until you cannot be together
    that you absolutely see them.
    The depth of their eyes,
    warmth of their smile,
    company that was kind to you.


It's not until you're unable to reach a person,
    that you truly appreciate them.
    Recounting time spent,
    knowing everything they meant
    and the memories keep finding you.


You may notice the repetition of the phrase, *it's not until*. There's also some internal rhyme and assonance present.


'Filling Station' by Elizabeth Bishop is freely available online and offers something poetic, out of the mundane offering of insight into working family life, using free verse.

. . .

The activity below will support you to plan, first draft and second draft a free verse poem.

[cwb 8.1] **Write about something that niggles you.**
Something that you have not been brave enough to write about yet, something that you would like to address. Go for it - this is a great chance to get something off your chest!

Free write, not worrying about punctuation, structure or even content. Give yourself ten minutes.

Go back through the piece and cross out any words or phrases that are not essential to the 'essence' of what you have written. Strip out anything that is not essential so that you are just left with a 'backbone.' What does the piece need to survive?

[cwb 8.2] **Rewrite your 'stripped back' version**, adding in anything that is required to strengthen your poem.

So, you've tried writing a few poem forms so far. Some of my favourite poetry collections house a variety of form and it's great to be as versatile a poet as possible.

9

––––––––

## FORM – TERZA RIMA

HERE'S another poem that is going to see you counting out syllables on your fingers! There are some fairly rigid 'rules' involved in writing a Terza Rima so even if this is the only time you ever write one, it will extend your range of skills as a poet.

The Terza Rima usually deals with subjects of love, loss or a **journey.** Like the sonnet, it uses ten syllables per line. There is no requirement for length – it can be as long or as short as it needs to be.

This Italian poetry form consists of stanzas of three lines (or tercets) usually in iambic pentameter, and follows an interlocking rhyming scheme, or chain rhyme. *'Acquainted with the Night'* by Robert Frost is an example of this form that can be found online. I have written several Terza Rimas and even now, I would find it impossible to write one without an example to follow!

. . .

**Structure** Right, you might need to read this sentence several times as it definitely takes some getting your head around... The middle line of each stanza rhymes with the <u>first and last</u> line of the each subsequent stanza.

There is no set length, as long as it follows the pattern below:

- **ABA** (first and third lines rhyme)
- **BCB** (first and third lines rhyme with middle line of previous tercet)
- **CDC** (first and third lines rhyme with middle line of previous tercet)
- **DED** (first and third lines rhyme with middle line of previous tercet)

Finally, the last stanza must be a couplet which rhymes with the middle line of the previous stanza. In this case, EE.

**Example - The Other Side**

In cold darkness, I gaze at this closed door A
   and ponder what might lie beyond its lure; B
   I haven't been as near and poised before, A
   So open to success but yet unsure, B
   my life spent entwined with this turmoil C
   where sense competes with freedom's fresh allure. B
   I'm so leaned on that, yes, I must recoil C

and swap stale air for oxygen around D
for no more of my years I want to spoil. C
I will be grateful that I walked new ground, D
one day beholden to the risk I faced E
and for fulfilment and the peace I've found. D
So this decision, from my gut I've based E
This, the final shut door that will be faced. E

[cwb 9.1] **It's your turn! Jot down notes, words, phrases, images, thoughts, etc about a <u>journey</u> you have taken.**

Include as much sensory information as possible. *What you saw, heard, felt etc.* Use these notes for your Terza Rima.

[cwb9.2] **Now write your first draft.**

It is advisable that you try to deal with your poem as it grows rather than trying to deal with it as a 'whole.'

Perhaps you could choose 'common' end rhyming words, for example 'night,' being that you will need to find three instances of each rhyme.

If 'night' was one of your end words, there are lots of words you can use with it, (sight, flight, plight, delight, light, height, etc.)

**10**

---

# FORM – THE VILLANELLE

THIS IS the last time in this book that I will have you writing to a definite form – I promise.

Of course, like me, you may really enjoy having rules in your writing, in which case, when I give you more freedom, starting in the next section, you can continue choosing to write in one of the forms we have covered.

We're now going to look at the 'Villanelle' poem, which means 'Irish Dance Song.' It was a form adopted by the French, but is becoming increasingly popular in England.

It is a highly structured poem, containing nineteen lines, two refrains and two repeating rhymes. The two refrains come together at the end of the poem. Does it sound complicated? It isn't, once you get into it. You've risen to the challenges so far so you can easily manage this one.

There's plenty of subjects to choose from as the Villanelle usually deals with subjects of love, loss or a challenge. Like the Sonnet and the Terza Rima, it *traditionally* uses ten syllables per line.

The **first and third** lines of the opening tercet are repeated alternately in the last lines of the subsequent stanzas. The middle line of each of the tercets rhymes. The refrains come back together for the two concluding lines. 'One Art' by Elizabeth Bishop is an example of this form and can be found online.

As with the Terza Rima, I wouldn't dream of trying to write one of these poems without an example of the structure at the side of my work in progress. Which is why I'll start by showing you an example that I've written.

## Example - Closing Doors

Loss needles at me as I say goodbye.
Onto these walls, I painted my dreams,
No amount of pain, could the colour hide.
A hopeful promise when I first arrived
will be carried forth by another, so it seems
Loss stabs at me as I say goodbye.
Warmth and comfort may have been mine,
now blinds cover where the sun should stream.
No amount of pain could the curtains hide.
Closing doors for the final time,
trying not to think what might have been.
Loss slices me as I say goodbye.
I recall the shouting that caused me to cry
I yearned to escape, to be safe and at peace,
No amount of pain could the music hide.
The flowers I planted will wither and die,
rotting into the ground before they've been seen.
Loss lays me to rest as I say goodbye.
No amount of pain could the colour hide.

. . .

Your turn now! [cwb10.1] **Jot down notes about a <u>loss</u> you have incurred at some point in your life.**

Include some information about setting and your feelings. This can be the loss of something tangible, such as a possession or it could deal with a loved one or a situation.

Poems with such tight structure can be constraining. On the other hand, when we have rules such as line and poem length, a poem can present itself to us as an 'empty vessel' just waiting to be filled with words and some poets (like me!) like this more than the freedom that a form like free verse offers.

Even if this is the only time you ever attempt a Villanelle, it will extend your technical abilities as a poet – I promise!

[cwb10.2] **Use your <u>loss</u> notes to weave into a Villanelle** which follows the story of the 'loss' you are writing about.

Think about which end rhymes you will use before you start as you will need to use them repeatedly.

You are best choosing 'line-end words where there are lots of words available, (e.g. night, light, fight or flower, hour, tower, etc.) You will notice from the example I gave you that the A end rhyme is used a lot.

Now we're at the end of this section, I can say it... The Villanelle is, in my opinion, one of the hardest poems to write, so when you've achieved it, give yourself a huge pat on the back. You'll only find out where you excel and what you enjoy about writing poetry by giving as many things as possible a try.

Well done! The next few sections are slightly less challenging in that they offer much more freedom, and you choose your own inspiration.

**11**

---

# WRITING FROM ART

POETRY AND ART can often be interlinked, as with all the arts, with each inspiring the other.

I like to think of a poem as painting a picture but by using our words instead of paint or pastilles. We should still be aiming to bring the picture to life as vividly as the artist has, for our readers.

Writing poetry from art is known as *Ekphrastic Poetry.* As a starting point, I like to imagine what might have inspired the artist. I am particularly drawn to art that tells a story, especially paintings featuring people. You, of course, will have your own preference.

**Choose a piece of artwork that inspires you.**

Use the prompts below to help you study your picture and make notes from which you can work.

. . .

[cwb 11.1] **Study your picture and make notes using the following prompts:**

- What senses are evoked? (sight, smell, touch, taste and sound.)
- Where is it set?
- What era is it? Time of year? Time of day?
- Who is in the picture – what relationships might exist between them?
- What is happening in the picture? What story is being told?
- How does the picture make you feel?

[cwb 11.2] **Now weave these notes into a first draft poem,** of any length, choosing from one of the forms we have looked at so far. (Free verse, sonnet, terza rima, villanelle, or a string of haiku or tankas.)

You are aiming for your reader to be able to visualise your picture after reading your poem.

As previously mentioned, we will revisit your piece further along in the course when we think about editing your work.

Continue to be alert to art all around you which might inspire further poems. You may become like me and see a poem in most pieces of artwork which you encounter!

**12**

---

# USING MUSIC AS INSPIRATION

As we started to consider in the last section, there is no doubt that different aspects of the arts interlink and inspire one another.

After considering paintings, we will now look at the influence *music* can have on poetry. And again you will have the same freedom as before, where you can respond by writing in the poetic form of your choice. I hope you are enjoying your new-found freedom!

1. Listen to a piece of classical music. This can be a favourite you already have, or the following piece is available online: Trois Gymnopedies (Orchestral) - Erik Satie (first piece.)

2. Listen to the piece a second time, making notes from the prompts below. **This will form the basis for the poem you will write.** [cwb 12.1]

- What words, phrases and images come into your mind as you listen to the piece?
- Could a story be being told?
- What is the mood?
- Can you associate any sounds, smells, feelings, sights or tastes?
- Does the music connect with you personally?
- What might be the era, time of day, time of year?

3. [cwb12.2] **Weave your notes and thoughts into a poem –** you choose the structure.

4. Read your poem aloud first without the music behind it and then with. The effect of the added music will amaze you.

We will return to it later in the course to give it another polish! You should now be starting to amass a sizeable pile of poems.

You can of course, write as many poems from each set of prompts and activities as you wish.

You will then finish up with either a more sizeable full-length collections or even two pamphlet sized ones. More on that later!

13

———

## USING ARTEFACTS AND
## OBJECTS AS INSPIRATION

As you are hopefully discovering, inspiration is all around us, and in this section you are going to use an object/artefact of personal significance to base your poem on.

It may be that you know the story behind what you have chosen, or it may be something beautiful or unique which you can bring to life for a reader to experience through a poem.

When I responded to this prompt myself, I chose a christening shawl crocheted by my great-great grandmother which had been passed through and down the family.

You too can choose a family heirloom as long as at it means something to you, for example, an ornament, a souvenir, a gift, jewellery, etc. You could even choose something much more ordinary as suggested below.

Read Carol Ann Duffy's poem 'Valentine,' which is available online. This originates from a very ordinary object, an onion.

.   .   .

[cwb13.1] **Work through the following prompts, making notes that will help you to formulate your poem.**

- What is your artefact and why have you made this choice?
- Describe what you have chosen (appearance, sound, smell, texture)
- What is its history?
- What might be the story behind it?
- Give some words that describe how it makes you feel?
- What words might you use in a poem about it?

[cwb13.2] **Now, use your notes to weave together a poem in a structure of your choice. It can be any length.**

This poem, like all the poems you have written so far, is best left to 'go cold' for at least two days after being first drafted. You can revisit it and either add to it or take bits out. There is a section on editing later in the book.

You should now be amassing a body of work which is building up to your collection. I hope you are feeling very proud of yourself!

Although the editing process is yet to be looked at, it is advisable to type up what you have worked on so far, make sure everything you have written is in one document.

## 14

## USING OWN EXPERIENCE
## AS INSPIRATION

WRITERS, especially poets, often bring their own experiences into their writing. I know I do! Everyone has their own story to tell and for new writers, this must often come out before more imaginative writing can be produced.

This can be for reasons of therapy, wanting to set a record straight, passing on a lesson learned or to consign something to print that will last forever.

An autography of an entire life is often told as prose. (Although Wordsworth wrote *The Prelude* – his life as a single poem, something I'd really like to try but feels like a mammoth undertaking!)

'Snapshots' into real life or a narrative autobiographical event are often recounted through verse and it is snapshots that are more manageable.

'*Birthday*' By Robinson Jeffers, (available online,) exemplifies this. You may also know of, or be able to find, other examples of autobiographical poetry.

. . .

The collections of poetry I have published so far are autobiographical although it is possible to disguise this – more on that in a moment.

[cwb 14.1] **Choose an autobiographical experience** you would like to portray through a poem, such as a relationship, a journey or an event.

Use the prompts below to decide on what will be contained within your poem.

- When did the episode take place?
- Was anyone else involved?
- What was the setting of your autobiographical experience?
- Bring it to life in a sensory way.
- How does the story begin?
- How does the story continue?
- How does the story end?
- What have you learned from the experience?
- How did it change you?
- What feelings can be attributed to it?
- What message would you like to convey to your readers?
- How should they feel after reading your poem?

[cwb 14.2] **Write your poem as a narrative with a beginning, middle and end, deciding on the structure yourself and whether it will rhyme.**

. . .

Ensure it ends on a reflective note showing the impact of the experience on you. Again, you are free to find your own way with this poem, in terms of form or free verse. You could also write in four-line verses, where the second and fourth lines rhyme.

If you also have the first and the third lines rhyming in a four-line verse, this is known as full rhyme. Or you could write in rhyming couplets, which, as the name suggests, is every two lines rhyming.

[cwb14.3] **Once you have completed the first draft of your poem, re-write it, changing the personal pronoun.**

So from (I, me, my) change to (s/he, her/him.) The result is twofold – first, if writing about something emotive or personal, changing the pronoun allows for some distance.

Second, this change somewhat removes you from the poem, allowing a reader to have greater accessibility to your work and as a result, more 'ownership' over the poem.

This is, I think, an exciting process. The poems belong to us as we create and perfect them but belong to the reader thereafter. They will likely make different stories and images from them. It is almost like an unwritten contract.

We give the most enjoyable and immersive reading experience we can for our reader, and provided we do this, they continue to read and recommend our work.

## 15

# WRITING LOVE POETRY – MAKING IT ORIGINAL

IN MY FACE to face classes, as soon as I say the words 'love poetry,' I am met with a groan! But love has been the number one subject of poetry since time began, so it has to be done!

However, most of it has all been done before so we have to find an original approach.

[cwb 15.1] **Write a list of commonly used symbols, words and phrases** that might find their way into a love poem. (e.g. heart, forever ...) These are words to be avoided or used sparingly when you come to write your poem.

Let us next consider what can make a love poem more unique, with particular regard to avoiding cliché or well-used words.

[cwb 15.2] **Find a love poem you enjoy and consider the following:**

- Why did you initially choose it?
- What do you like about it?
- Can you identify with it?
- What is different about it compared to other love poetry?
- Say something about the form and structure of it.

**Writing from your own experience** can assure the likelihood of an original and unique poem. However, if you are completely balking at this idea, choose something other than 'romantic' love. One writer I worked with chose the subject of running. Another chose a family member.

[cwb 15.3] **Whoever or whatever you choose, respond to the prompts below as a starting point for your love poem.**

1. *Who* (or what!) are you going to write about?
2. Decide on your *tone* – will it be positive, negative, funny, etc.
3. Choose some *words and phrases* to describe the object of your poem.
4. Talk about when you *first met them*. What details can you recall?
5. Compare your life *before* and *after* they had a role in your life story.
6. What is <u>*different*</u> about your experience to other people's?
7. What *message* would you like to resonate from your poem?

[cwb 15.4] **Use your notes to write the first draft of your poem, letting it find its own form.**


Enjoy your reminiscences – you didn't honestly think you were going to get through this course without having to write a love poem, did you?!

# 16

# USING METAPHOR AND SIMILE

Similes and metaphors are very much part of a writer's 'toolbox,' whether in poetry or prose. I try to use one in most of my poems, where they are available and appropriate.

They are powerful in that the object or thing that is being used in the comparison is often very distinct to the reader, so that they can imagine what the writer is trying to convey.

For example, *'My love is a red, red rose.'* Everybody knows what a rose looks like and that it is vibrant, sleek, fragrant and beautiful. They should therefore be easily able to equate that vision with what 'love' is.

Similes and metaphors should be used to convey a distinct image whilst being used sparingly. It is also important that they are original – which is the difficult part!

Often, if you can use something that is personal to you, that is more likely to guarantee originality, for example, in one of my poems I wrote a line using the following metaphor:

*When we were inseparable, like a polished, new pair of shoes.*

This was an observation which had come to me whilst

looking at shoes and it is these personal observations that will grant you individuality.

An example of simile being used in poetry is 'Men are like buses' by Wendy Cope. An example of metaphor being used in poetry is 'The Force' by Dylan Thomas. Both poems are available online.

[cwb16.1] **What is a Simile?**

What words are used within the sentence that tell us a phrase is a simile?Can you think of an example of a simile?

[cwb16.2] **What is a Metaphor?**

Can you think of an example of a metaphor?

Warning! The next two challenges are much harder than they first appear...

[cwb16.3] **Here are three cliché similes – can you improve them by offering an original alternative?**

1. As hard as nails
2. Like two peas in a pod
3. As light as a feather

[cwb16.4] **Here are three cliché metaphors – can you improve them by offering an original alternative?**

1. It was music to his ears
2. Life is a roller coaster

3. The world is a stage

[cwb16.5] **Choose one of these <u>improved versions</u> or a simile/metaphor of your own to inspire a poem that could be used within your collection.**

The line should appear in its entirety somewhere in your poem or as the title.

# 17

## HALFWAY THERE!

Congratulations, you are at the halfway point of this book with lots of new poems to your name.

**Now is a good time to focus on what you have achieved so far, and what work still needs to be done.** [cwb 17.1]

1. Can you say in a maximum of two sentences, what your collection is about?
2. What does it have that makes it different from other collections?
3. What are you most proud of in relation to your collection so far?
4. What is your main strength as a poet?
5. Who would you like to read your work?
6. What will be your overall title?
7. What do you imagine your book jacket looking like?
8. How many poems do you imagine your completed collection containing?

9.  How many of them have you written so far?
10. What is yet to be done?
11. Now you have a 'body of work' emerging, how would you describe your voice and style as a poet?
12. How will you feel when you hold your completed collection in your hands?

I hope that responding to the above questions has helped with your sense of accomplishment so far.

You're doing great – keep going – it won't be too long before people are queuing up for a signed copy!

**18**

———

# SHAPE POETRY

As WELL AS providing resonance and being audibly pleasing, we can also consider the physical appearance of a poem on the page.

Some poets enjoy writing shape poetry and they certainly offer an extra dimension when presented amongst your free verse, sonnets and villanelles!

A shape poem is written in the shape of its subject. As an example, I have written one about the passage of time in the shape of a sand timer, as shown below:

Other possibilities are: *Pieces of clothing, a country, an object, a heart, a building, an animal, an ascension, a descent.*

There are many examples available online, such as *The Mouse's Tale* by Lewis Carroll.

**19**

___

# THE SAND TIMER

The constant flow can neither
be slowed or stopped,
rich in past choices,
former tears and loss.
It can't be turned over,
this life which exists
A knowing that there's
more to living than this.
Sand pooled below me
Can never be
lessened or changed.
I look up
and ahead,
wondering
what might
remain.
Has
more life
trickled through
than is left behind

or perhaps running out
so I have to find
what happens if I just
let go and be, following dreams,
feeling happy and free.
Instead of looking down, feeling
regret and bereft, I am in control
of the sand that is left.

DECIDE on the subject and shape for your shape poem.


[cwb 18.1] **Make notes of words, images and phrases.**


[cwb 18.2] **Write the first draft of your poem.**


[cwb 18.3] **Then shape it.**

**20**

---

# LANDSCAPE POETRY

IN THE SAME way as the 'writing from art' activity, landscape poetry, should aim to bring to life a vision for the reader, again, as though painting a picture, but using words instead of a paintbrush.

Some wonderful poetry has been inspired by landscape. If you are an artist or photographer in addition to your writing talent, you could produce an entire collection or pamphlet on landscape alone.

[cwb19.1] **Consider the following:**

- What is landscape poetry? What does this phrase mean to you as a reader and as a poet?
- What sort of places can be written about?
- Which famous poets are known for their landscape poetry?
- Why is landscape said to be inspiring?
- What might a landscape poet be hoping to achieve in their work?

[cwb19.2] **Respond to the prompts below** in order that you can really 'find your way' into your landscape to poetically convey it. You could work from a memory of your chosen landscape, or from a picture. The best practice would be to visit the landscape itself and write directly from within it.

**Use your memory, picture or experience to consider the following:**

Jot down some notes about what can be:

- *Seen:*
- *Heard:*
- *Felt:*
- *Smelt and:*
- *Tasted:*
- How does the landscape make you feel?
- What is happening within your landscape?
- What time of year/day is it?
- Could a story be being told?
- How do you want your reader to feel after reading this poem?
- Give your landscape a title – you may use this as the title of your poem?

[cwb19.3] **Weave the above information into the first draft of a poem, using whichever structure and form you choose.** Try to make sure your reader will be able to visualise your landscape when reading it.

Remember you are painting your landscape, but with words.

## 21

# INVERTED POETRY

AN 'INVERTED' poem offers the reader something different – it is a poem that goes in reverse and tells a story *backwards.*

It can be helpful to firstly note the possible content of your poem, words, phrases, images and ideas, and write it 'forwards' before switching it around and writing it backwards.

Read the example below, *'Her Undoing.'* This begins at the point of the woman's 'date' not arriving and works backwards to the moment of being 'asked out.' I actually wrote this poem from a painting – it is not based on experience!

**Her Undoing**

Soaking up tears,
    un-ordering the wine,

a bag swinging from her arm,
she would never have arrived.
Butterflies calm,
heart-rate slowed,
the black dress on the hanger
and bracelet adorning its box.
No blusher dusted, lipstick unapplied,
no perfume ever sprayed,
lashes uncurled,
hair hanging loose around her shoulders.
Hope not being allowed to shower
as her outfit planned,
that would not be worn,
not this night.
She would un-answer the call,
forget his smile
and never have heard his voice.


[cwb 20.1] **Take one of the poems you have yet to write for your collection** – one that tells 'a story' and jot down some notes which follow how they would progress in a natural sequential order. (Just notes at this stage.)

Themes such as an event that can be narrated, or some aspect of time, (e.g. the ageing process,) lend themselves to be worked in this way.


[cwb 20.2] **Using 'Her Undoing' as a 'model,' write your own poem as an 'inversion' of events.**

.  .  .

It might help to write your poem 'forwards' first and then reverse it.

Using time connectives like 'next,' 'before' and 'finally' can offer structure and can be partially or wholly removed at editing stage if preferred.

Your collection, by now, should be demonstrating your versatility as a poet, offering a variety of form, and inspiration, and with the poems you've recently written, such as shape and inversion – something very unique.

# 22

# EXTENDED PERSONIFICATION WITHIN A POEM

'PERSONIFICATION' in poetry is taking something that is not human and personifying it by giving it human qualities. It is synonymous with metaphor in that it is saying something is something else.

- The fire swallowed the entire forest.
- The clouds pushed each other around in the sky.
- Winter's icy grip squeezed his rib cage.
- The silence crept into the classroom.

Personification is the giving of human qualities to inanimate objects. The above examples of personification show that this literary device helps to relate the 'actions' of inanimate objects to our own emotions.

Extended personification occurs *where instead of just a single statement being used, e.g. 'we are branches on a tree,' the idea is continued for the duration of a poem.*

. . .

Emotions and experiences are commonly personified within a poem – saying something is something else can be used to almost hide behind and provide distraction from a personal element of a poem. For example, the 'black dog' has been used to personify depression.

'Objects' that could be personified in poetry are: animals, things in nature, items of clothing, transport. And I'm sure you can think of many more!

Below is an example where 'extended personification' has been used to represent the ocean. A further example can be found online – *Mirror* by Sylvia Plath.

**The Hunter**

All blue-eyed and innocent,
    it endeavours to fool,
    murmuring sweet-nothings
    alluring, outwardly swollen
    with life and breath,
    perhaps resentful
    of all truly alive.
    Glib on the surface,
    concealing what's beneath;
    deviously waiting
    for its prey.
    No mercy will be afforded

to those who succumb.
They will be snatched
between laughing jaws
of foaming venom.
Churned and tossed
till the final gasp;
condemned to the depths.
A fresh dawn glows,
granting reprieve.
All seems forgotten,
an obscure memory now.
The ocean reclines without conscience,
observing, misleading, all blue-eyed and innocent.


[cwb 21.1]**Choose an emotion or experience you would like to convey through your poem.** (e.g. revenge, loneliness)


[cwb 21.2] **What inanimate object are you going to use to represent it?**


[cwb 21.3] **What features of that object can you use?** (e.g. to talk about the experience of divorce, a 'corpse' could be used as a metaphor – the features that might be used could be cold, lifeless, still, toxic, etc.)


[cwb 21.4] **Weave your notes into your first draft, letting your poem find its own form.**

. . .

I think this is one of the most difficult activities in this book, so take your time with it, and please accept an advance pat on the back for its completion!

**23**

---

# KEEPING THE READER IN
# MIND WHILST WRITING

LOTS OF POEMS you write will be for yourself when you are trying to make sense of life. There is no doubt that writing is therapeutic. Difficult experiences and troubling life events can can be explored. Many will never see the light of day – or so you may think!

I have had a couple of 'personal' collections published containing poems that I never thought would end up out there but your troubles now can be someone else's solution later.

When you are writing with the aim of any sort of publication or for an audience, you should keep your readers in mind, balancing this with staying true to yourself and your inner voice as a poet.

It can help to have an idea of a 'typical' ideal reader, who might be interested in your collection.

(Age, gender, geographical location, interests, experiences.)

. . .

[cwb 22.1] **Write a letter to your ideal reader, telling them what they can expect from your collection, the effect you hope it has on them and anything else you would like to say.**

The following suggestions will assist you as you continue writing poems with a potential reader in mind.

[cwb 22.2] **Keep the points below in mind as you continue with your collection, and throughout the editing process for each poem.**

- What might draw a reader to a particular poem?
- Is the poem 'saying' something and taking the reader on a journey?
- What is unique about the poem?
- What overall message do you want the poem to convey?
- Who might it speak to?
- What experience might your reader be seeking from the reading of your poem? (e.g. comfort, advice.)

You should apply the above questions to each of the poems you have written so far, but for now, **relate it to the first draft of your next poem.** [cwb 22.3]

Below are some other ways to make your poems accessible to your readers:

1. Set your location in a universal place, rather than an exact location (e.g. not Lake Windermere or Rowntree's Park. Make it general instead, e.g. a lake, a park, a river, a kitchen.
2. If you have written the piece using first person

narrative, switch it into third person. This is a really powerful way of distancing yourself from your work.

3. Do lots of 'showing,' rather than 'telling.' For example, instead of saying 'it is autumn,' describe the colours. Or instead of saying 'I felt safe,' talk about your surroundings wrapping their arms around you.

**24**

# EDITING POETRY AND TIGHTENING WRITING

THE TERM EDITING means making your poem the best it can be – *improving,* rather than *creating.* Ensuring each word has earned its place in your poem.

The term tightening writing means *omitting words that do not need to be there.*

Take a poem from your collection so far – a printed out version is best, in double lined spacing with plenty of room around it for annotations.

1. Read your poem aloud.
2. Next, annotate your poem, referring to the editing checklist below and noting wordiness, word choices, superfluous words and any other possibilities you find needing improvement.
3. Amend your original work. This would be a good time to compare your before and after versions in the light of what you have changed and the effect it has had.
4. Read it aloud again.

<u>Editing Checklist</u>

- Has the poem started in the right place? Sometimes writers begin a poem too early, giving too much description, scene setting or backstory. Launch straight in at a point of interest.
- Similarly, have you laboured your ending? End it succinctly at a point of reflection.
- Read your poem out loud. This highlights repeated words.
- Whilst reading aloud, check for places of natural pause, where commas or extra full stops might be necessary.
- Have you 'over-written' anywhere? Are there places where you have used two similar adjectives or verbs where one 'stronger' one would suffice? Stronger verbs can ensure you show, rather than tell.
- Beware of overusing adjectives – use them sparingly as they can clutter up a poem.
- Look out for superfluous words like very, so, just, that, etc. Removal of these makes a poem stronger.
- Consider removal of anything not essential to a poem's backbone.
- Are you saying the same thing twice anywhere? (I do this a lot!)
- Has every word earned a place in your poem? Consider using a thesaurus to improve your poem's vocabulary or use the synonyms function on your computer. ('Right click' on a word then select an alternative from the drop-down menu.)
- If when reading your work aloud, you are tripping

over words or they seem a bit 'clunky,' think about
altering so the piece reads more smoothly.
- Allow your poem to go cold for a day or two before
returning to it with fresh eyes.
- Check for continuity – make sure the viewpoint or
tense doesn't suddenly slip.
- Show your poem to a reader or another writer,
inviting them to apply the above principles to your
work. Often you become too close to a poem and
cannot see what someone else might.

Go through another of your poems again using the editing
checklist.

Begin collating the work you have so far into one folder. (Both
on your computer and in print.)

Continue the editing process with each of the poems you are
intending to include in your collection. This is a lengthy process,
so I would recommend only editing a poem or two a day.

**25**

---

## PUTTING IT ALL TOGETHER – ASSEMBLING AND ORDERING YOUR WORK

THROUGHOUT THE COURSE, you have amassed a considerable body of poetry – something to congratulate yourself for.

If you have written one poem from each section in this book, you will be working on a pamphlet sized collection, ideal for a debut poet, but if you've written one poem per week, you will be able to create a full length collection, often a more attractive proposition for publishers.

Now you can decide on the order of your collection and how it will be organised. There are three main ways:

1. **Chronologically** – an order which tells of a journey, story or time-related episode, forwards or backwards.
2. **Contrasted** – mixing up voices, forms, tone and mood. Light against dark. Fast against slow. Structured form against free verse.

3.  **Divided into Sections** – poems are divided into
    clearly demarcated sections, by subject, theme or
    tone.

[cwb 23.1] **Write a first draft, encapsulating your book's essence in a few lines for the 'blurb' on the back cover** – you write this to entice a reader, as opposed to the 'endorsements,' which third parties write. Look at some published poetry books for ideas of tone and length.

This is a very individual aspect and not all poetry books include one. Though the more features your book displays to help it to sell, the better.

[cwb 23.2] **Work through the prompts below.** They will help you make decisions about the structure of your collection.

1.  Title and subtitle of your book:
2.  Theme(s):
3.  What 'threads' run through the collection – make
    notes on how your poems are either similar or
    different to each other.
4.  How will you decide on the order? Consider
    chronology, groupings or contrasted.
5.  Will it be split into parts? Will each part be titled?
6.  Arrange your poems into a 'draft' order, (easier when
    choosing from physical print outs of each poem.)

It's all starting to come together now! You should be feeling excited and proud of yourself. I hope you have been telling everyone you know what you are working on – they will be queueing up for a signed copy!

**26**

---

# TYPESETTING, PRESENTATION AND PERFECTING YOUR MANUSCRIPT

WHETHER YOU WANT to submit your poetry to a magazine, publisher or publish your collection independently, consistent presentation is essential.

Look at some published collections of poetry and make notes on presentational features. Apply these principles to your own work, also using the guidance given below.

Ensure that each of your selected poems is correctly ordered within a single continuous word document – one poem per page. Or use consecutive pages for longer poems. Use the title of your book as the filename.

Ensure each of your poems is in a uniform format. You can just 'select' the entire file before changing the font, line spacing etc, to do it all at once. Also make sure your pages are numbered.

·　·　·

## Contents Page

Produce an accurate contents page.

## Personalisation

[cwb 24.1] This is the time when you can write dedications, acknowledgements and a short author biography that makes you relatable to your intended readers.

**Include information such as where you come from, how long you've been writing, what has inspired your collection and what you hope your reader will experience as a result of it.**

## Titles

Poem titles are not usually published <u>underlined</u> or UPPERCASE. However, they are often **bold,** in Title Case or lowercase. Ensure they are consistent; for example don't have 'the' in one title, and 'The' in the next. Some poets choose a larger font size for titles.

## Alignment

Left align your poems. Only centre or right align for effect or symmetry, (e.g. a shape poem.)

## Font

Make sure the font is legible, (e.g. Times New Roman or Aerial,) 11 point is usual in poetry collections. Again, be consistent, i.e. use the same font for all poems.

.   .   .

**Margins**

Standard margin size on A4 is 2.54cm on all sides.


**Line length**

Manage your line length in accordance with the likely format of publication. Most will be published A5 or smaller. If you are in the habit of writing on A4 with long lines the line breaks will change on publication.


*Ensure your manuscript is **flawless!***


Continue writing anything that still needs including, editing and presenting your work.

## 27

# NETWORKING AS A POET–OPEN MICS AND OTHER EVENTS

BEING a professional writer isn't solely about the act of writing, but also about the immersion of yourself within the world of writing - giving yourself the opportunity to put yourself and your work out there.

Writing can be a solitary activity, sometimes even a lonely one. This can be alleviated by seeking out the company of other like-minded people.

The writing world offers lots of opportunities for networking and keeping abreast of everything going on in the world of writing.

**Literature Festivals**

These are commonly held in March and October and feature talks by established writers, and workshops.

. . .

**Writing Conferences**

You will probably get the most benefit out of these when approaching publication or just afterwards. They tend to be more expensive than festivals but usually feature keynote speakers and information sessions.

They provide a brilliant opportunity for mingling with other writers and professionals in the writing industry.


**Open Mic Events**


**There are several advantages of attending spoken word events:**

- Being able to showcase your work and yourself as a poet.
- Becoming part of a community and network of writers.
- Living as a writer and improving confidence.
- Listening and watching the styles of other poets and becoming more familiar with poetic trends.
- Being less isolated as a writer.
- Practice with reading to an audience. (Think of your book launch!)

**Nerves can be a problem, however: below are a few tips on how to overcome them.**

- Foremost, knowing that the work you are going to read is the best it can be.
- Become familiar with the use of a microphone before the event.

- Rehearsing it at home, possibly in front of a mirror and timing your performance. Take note of any occasions where you stumble over words.
- Going 'first' can make you feel as though you are getting it out of the way but by listening to several other poets before it is your turn, you give yourself time to focus outside yourself and get a feel for the theme and content.
- This time can also be used for regulating your breathing.

**Whilst reading:**

- Ensure your position is comfortable and the right distance in relation to the microphone.
- Remember to breathe!
- Read your work slowly and clearly, pausing where necessary to allow the words to sink in – overcome the temptation to rush.
- Imagine yourself as a 'vehicle' for the poem – as though the words are emerging from behind you and are just travelling through you, to meet your audience.
- Pause as and when necessary to allow audience reaction. (For example, if reading anything particularly funny or resonant.)
- Allow for applause in between your poems, if reading several.
- Look up from your page every so often – look out across your audience.
- Hold a book or a folder containing your poem – the 'shakes' will be less obvious.

- Ensure you read a poem where the audience will be in no doubt as to where it ends. You might want to say 'thank you' at the end of the final poem.
- Congratulate yourself afterwards and remember it will not always be so nerve wracking – all poets have to read for the first time somewhere! Writers are generally a friendly and supportive community.

[cwb 25.1] **Choose two or three of your own poems** that would be suitable for performance.

You will need to be discerning; some poems are best 'off' the page and others, perhaps ones that include lots of auditory features, (rhyme, alliteration, consonance and assonance,) are better read aloud.

Content is an important consideration. Some poems 'go down' better than others with an audience. Humour can be good, as can poems of a topical theme. Choose poems that are accessible and interesting, as well as something that will be understood easily.

Remember that the audience can only grasp what they hear, they will not have a copy to visually follow as you read.

**Using the guidance given above, practise reading them aloud** several times before timing yourself. Usually at open mic events, you are given a three to five minute reading slot. It's up to you whether you read a longer piece or two or three shorter ones.

. . .

You may also find it helpful to record your reading on a phone or webcam then play it back to hear if there is any occasion of stumbling over words, etc.

You could also read in front of someone else to get a feel for having someone listen to you and for their feedback.

28

———

# CREATING AN ON-LINE
# AUTHOR PLATFORM

AN AUTHOR PLATFORM has two elements; the *offline* one which consists of real, physical writing communities you can belong to, such as writing groups and writers circles, or literary events you attend, as mentioned in the last section.

Then there is the *online* element which consists of social media, blogging and having a website. This section will address these aspects.

Your author platform is primarily about recognition of your name, and secondly about recognition of your books.

## What is an Author Platform?

It is an on-line identity that will enable potential readers, agents and publishers, to recognise your name, whether you use your real name or a pseudonym.

Therefore you will need to think carefully about how you want to present yourself to the world and how much of yourself you want to reveal.

80

A platform offers assurance to publishers and agents that you already have a 'following,' who may become potential readers. It also demonstrates the ability to promote yourself.

If you want to be discovered as a writer, you *must* have a web presence. If Google searches can find you, you become more of a contender in the writing world.

The information given below is not exhaustive but is an indication of the *minimum* you should establish for an effective on-line presence.

## Create a Facebook, Twitter or Instagram Account

Facebook, Twitter and Instagram are amongst the fastest ways to gain a presence in cyber space. They provide access to thousands of people. Use them to gain 'friends' and followers. You can also choose to follow things and people that interest you.

Being active on one or more of these online social networks will allow you to promote your poetry collection once it is completed. Being on a platform will also help you to stay informed of events and writing opportunities, such as competitions or submission opportunities.

You should 'link' any social media you are part of to your website – more on that in a moment. Personally, I favour Facebook, but this is an individual decision.

***Get started before submitting to a publisher!!***

- Create your social media account(s.)

- You may decide just to have your presence associated with your identity as a writer so you may wish to act under your pen name, if you have one. I advise keeping your personal profile separate and creating a separate writer persona.
- You will have to upload a picture of yourself and complete the info page, remember you only need to give as much information as you want the world to know and can keep that completely linked to yourself as a writer.
- Start to add mutual friends and followers. Follow or send friend requests to writers you know or have met, (note down names at events you attend.)
- Within this you can include other authors, publishers, agents, events, or magazines.
- Soon, when you view your 'news feed,' you will be receiving news of events and opportunities, as well as information on the work of your fellow writers. You can join in with this, offering comments and encouragement to others, as well as beginning to promote yourself.
- You need to be logging into your social media account regularly, at least three times a week if possible, to accept friend requests, interact with others, and keep in touch with everything that is going on in the world of writing.

**Create a Website**

Your website should include your profile as a writer and link to your social media channels. You should use the same photo and identity to create your own online branding.

After you have been published, you can add book covers of your own work or anthologies you're included in, linking to other websites or Amazon pages.

Your website should include a contact form and a 'blog.' You may wish to include short examples of your writing, (but be careful here,) because posting work in the public domain can render it already published.

A website is fairly static in that you probably will not need to update it much, but a blog (essentially an on-line diary,) will need updating regularly. You can blog about anything, your experiences as a writer, a regular activity you do, or know a lot about - parenting, politics or whatever think will attract regular readers.

The closer it is linked to the theme of your poetry collection, the better, but do keep in mind that you might want to promote future publications, so you won't want your blog to be too niche.

A blog in itself, will eventually gain a following and people can interact with you and leave comments for you and others. It will not only invite people to your website, which will potentially increase future book sales, it will also showcase your ability to write and allow you to sound your voice as a writer.

You could add a video, (using a YouTube link,) to your website. This enables a publisher or potential reader to actually see you. Here you could include a book trailer, you reading your work or a writer interview. I repurpose all my blog posts as YouTube videos.

A good place to start is the websites of other writers, however, at least to start with, keep your own website as simple as possible. Wordpress is probably the simplest platform on which to build your site but there are lots of others. I do recommend Wordpress though – it's inexpensive, has a good level of support and if I can work my way through it... well, I'm no technical expert, at all!

It can be a fiddly process but the more you feel your way through it, the better you will get and the more enjoyable it will become.

It is possible to pay to have these on-line services established for you, but there is lots of step-by-step guidance around that will help you build your own and I would argue that it is best to learn the processes of the platforms you're working with from the ground up yourself. That way, once you're in a position to outsource this responsibility, you will know exactly what is entailed and what you are paying for.

Ultimately publishers will be interested in you having a social media presence with as many followers as possible. They may ask questions around website traffic so include a visitor counter as you are setting it up.

The main drawback to all of the above is obviously the time that is involved in getting up and running, and then maintaining contacts and updates. But there is no doubt that building a platform will make you more part of the writing community, it will increase sales of your poetry collection when it is ready, and it will open new doors for you as a poet.

It will take effort, particularly to start with but the importance of a well-planned and implemented author platform cannot be emphasised enough.

[cwb 26.1] **Choose one aspect of building your online presence and take your first steps towards getting it up and running.**

---

# 29

# PUBLISHING – TRADITIONAL
# AND INDEPENDENT

THIS IS what you've been working towards. After completing your collection, you are hopefully seeking publishing success, whether that is finding a traditional publisher or publishing independently.

Most debut poets are wise to set their sights on having smaller successes first, in poetry competitions and anthologies.

Winning or being shortlisted increases your chances of being accepted by a publisher. These achievements give you an edge over poets submitting their manuscripts who have none.

The other advantage of submission to competitions and anthologies is the requirement to submit by a deadline, as well as possibly having to work to set parameters like a word count, line count or theme. These all help develop disciplines needed to be a successful writer.

You could consider regularly entering your work, perhaps every fortnight or every month to increase your chances, keeping a record of all your submissions.

. . .

## Anthologies

Inclusion in an anthology is a great way to start building up your writing CV and if you're lucky, will involve an invite to a book launch event. This, as we've talked about before, will raise your profile as a poet and allow a networking opportunity.

There are many regular publications that invite poetry submissions from established and emerging poets. A Google search, or one of the monthly or quarterly writing magazines will offer details of anthologies inviting submissions.

## Competitions

Good for building up a history of success but often carry an entry fee, and the free ones tend to be saturated with entries. Still, very worth a go, as being short-listed, even long-listed, is deemed a success when you're selling yourself as a poet. There are always plenty of competitions and again, a Google search or one of the monthly or quarterly magazines will offer details of current poetry competitions.

Once your poetry collection is edited, you have the choice of one of the following publication avenues.

## Publishers

You may be thinking about submitting a pamphlet for publication, (18-30 poems.) If you've a larger body of work, you may be considering sending in a full length collection, (45 poems upwards.)

There are two types of publisher you can submit to. The first are the national publishing companies, mostly based in London. However, the publishers most likely to take a chance on new talent are the independent publishing houses, (aka indie publishers.) Whether you choose a smaller or larger publisher to offer your collection to, you should visit their website and carefully follow their submission guidelines.

Full listings of all UK and overseas poetry publishers are given in the Writers and Artist's Yearbook, published each year, and well worth owning, although all libraries hold a reference copy.

The advantages of being accepted by a publisher are that they will undertake many aspects of what is required to make your collection the best it can be, such as editing , formatting and cover design. They will also have a marketing budget and plenty of expertise.

Having said that, publishers usually only get behind their writers in terms of marketing for the short term and marketing responsibility is increasingly on you, as the poet. A publisher will also take at least 20% of profits and some operate with contract terms that include a complete royalty split.

**Independent Publishing**

You could opt to cut out the 'gatekeepers,' (competitions and publishers,) and get your work straight in front of your readers. There are normally some associated costs in publishing, but you keep hold of a greater percentage of the profit.

Kindle Direct Publishing offers a 35% royalty, (70% if you

enrol your book into Kindle Unlimited.) You can produce your book as a paperback and as an e-book, and can order a box of author copies at cost price, to sell directly to your family and friends, and at any launch events of promotions you organise.

The following points need to be kept in mind when publishing independently:

- Your writing must be polished and edited, (preferably professionally.)
- You should consider having the book cover professionally designed.
- You will need to research the formatting process.
- You will need a budget for Amazon ads and/or Facebook ads to get your work in front of readers.

[cwb 27.1] **Decide on what step forward in terms of publishing you would like to take and begin to research it.**

**30**

---

# YOUR COVER LETTER

If you are planning to approach a publisher, your cover letter is a vital part of your submission package.

[cwb 28.1] **The notes you will make in response to the following prompts** will provide you with a basis from which to write your covering letter. This will be adapted according to the requirements of each publisher you submit to.

- A summary of your collection in two lines. (The elevator pitch – imagine someone stopping you in the street and asking you what your collection is about.)

For example, the pitch for my collection – 'Poetry for the Newly Married 40 Something,' would be:

*A collection of poetry that explores dating in your forties and how to get from Tinder to altar!*

. . .

- Why you have written your collection. (Relevant expertise or experience, inspirations and motivations.)
- Who it might be of interest to? (Who might be your typical reader: age, gender, demographic, interests, etc.)
- Comparable works or poets. (Are there any poets or collections whose style, voice or subject you feel close to?)
- What poets you like to read and have influenced you. (Your response to this demonstrates that you have some understanding of the market.)
- Previous publications and successes in your writing. (This is where your writing 'CV' comes in. Any longlists, shortlists, inclusions or wins should be included here.)
- Events and courses you attend/have attended. (This demonstrates your commitment to your professional development and the honing of your writing craft.)
- Any other relevant biographical information. Really sell yourself here – this is no time to hide your light under a bushel! At the end of your letter, you could add a personal touch by stating why you have chosen them, as a publisher, to approach.

[cwb 28.2] **Now use these responses to draw together the first draft of your cover letter.**

# 31

# YOUR NEXT WRITING STEPS

Now that you've reached the end of this course, you will have gained new skills, confidence, and hopefully a writing discipline.

It could be helpful to consider where you go from here. Below are a few suggestions, drawn from the last sections of the course.

- Subscription to a writing or poetry magazine – this will keep you informed of opportunities and events, whilst being an excellent source for continued learning.
- Open mic nights – great for networking and building your confidence as a writer.
- Building your author platform - (social media, website, blog, etc) – give yourself plenty of time to work on it, but don't let it take you away from your writing.
- Attend further courses – look out for workshops at literature festivals and writing days. You may want to

aim even higher and consider an OU, BA or MA in Creative Writing or other accredited course.

- Attend literature festivals. They tend to be widely held in March and October. Packed with workshops and inspirational speakers, they also usually hold a competition and offer networking opportunities.
- Keep making submissions – submit a poem or three to a magazine or to a competition on a regular basis. Perhaps each week or each month. This will build up your writing CV.
- Join a writing group or find a 'writing buddy.' Writing can be a lonely and solitary activity, therefore joining an established writing group or meeting regularly with a writing friend can be an excellent way to stay connected to other writers. It also offers the opportunity to help one another and provide feedback to one another. If there isn't one in your area, consider starting one of your own. Other local writers will love you for doing this.
- Manuscript appraisal – if you have not already done so, consider having your poetry manuscript professionally critiqued, edited and proofread. At the very least, have a 'writing buddy' or trusted reader look over it. Make sure you have got it to the best place you can before you consider publication.

[cwb 29.1] **Consider what you want to have achieved in the next month, three months, six months, etc.** Be specific and realistic. Give yourself targets.

These could be related to your writing craft or to your professional development. Ensure each goal is Specific, Measurable, Attainable, Realistic and Timed. (S.M.A.R.T.)

. . .

You have now completed 'Write a Collection of Poetry in a Year.' Well done!

Your final instruction is to raise a glass in celebration of all your hard work and achievement. Keep it up and happy editing!

I'd love to know what you thought of Write a Collection of Poetry in a Year. The easiest way to do this is by leaving a review, and you can leave one by revisiting the retailer from whom you bought this book. It's great to know what you want more of, or not, as the case may be! It only needs to be a line or three, but also helps other writers find the book.

**Thank you!**

# HOW-TO BOOKS FOR WRITERS

Write your Life Story in a Year
Write a Novel in a Year
Write a Collection of Poetry in a Year
Write a Collection of Short Stories in a Year

# INTERVIEW WITH THE AUTHOR

**Q: When did you start writing?**

A: I've been making up stories and poems since I was able to hold a pen but only in my forties was I able to make it my full-time career.

**Q: What do you write?**

A: Mainly dark domestic thriller novels. But I also have a memoir, two collections of poetry, a short story collection and four how-to books for writing.

**Q: What do other writers say about you?**

A: That my books and courses offer an accessible and supportive route to writers who have a dream to achieve. Also, that I'm an inspirational and motivating teacher of creative writing.

**Q: What's the best thing about being a writer?**

A: My lovely readers. AND being part of an awesome community of writers. Hearing from readers and other writers absolutely makes my day!

**Q: Who are you and where are you from?**

A: A born 'n' bred Yorkshire lass, with two grown up sons and a Sproodle called Molly. (Springer/Poodle!) The last decade has been the best: I've done an MA in Creative Writing, made writing my full time job, and found the happy-ever-after that doesn't exist in my writing - after marrying for the second time just before the pandemic.

**Q: What qualifies you to deliver courses on creative writing?**

A: I have a teaching degree and a Masters in Creative Writing. I also enjoy a large and regular readership for the books I have written and favourable reviews of my work.

**Q: How it is possible to achieve success as a writer?**

A: *Keep going, keep writing, keep believing in your voice.* The really exciting thing is that writing is something you will only ever get better and better at.

# ACKNOWLEDGMENTS

I'd like to say a huge thank you to my husband, Michael, for his support in the latter stages of this book.

Thanks also to all the writers who have taken this course over the years, either in the classroom or by distance learning. Your feedback has enabled me to tweak and refine the course, and many of you have become friends too!

Thank you to Prince Henry's Grammar School in Otley for the space and platform for me to offer my creative writing courses, and I also want to acknowledge Leeds Trinity University where I completed my teaching and English degree, and then my Masters in Creative Writing.

These degrees took me to a new level as a writer and enabled me to pass on my own learning through the courses I've written and now offer.

And lastly, can I thank you, the 'student' of this book, for choosing to share your writing journey with me, and for allowing me to share what I know to help you write your own poetry collection. It is a true honour and I hope you will keep me posted of your success!

www.ingramcontent.com/pod-product-compliance
Lightning Source LLC
Chambersburg PA
CBHW031750150726
47989CB00006B/2663